Through his debut full-length collection *The Hours*, Matthew J. Andrews unflinchingly explores aspects of God and a faithful life that are painful, weighty, and even violent. Andrews' imaginative—but not sentimental!—gaze shows us Christ's body "chopped like onions" through the Eucharist; the angel Gabriel's feathered wings as "a train of candles / settled in a prolonged burn"; and King David's desperation for God to speak in "a tone that is not thunder, / in a voice that is not rain." These poems and the elusive God they seek to meet (or sometimes avoid) have a satisfying sting to them. *The Hours* does not dismiss or denigrate the biblical stories it references or their God, but instead unveils the complex realities of these inspirations and of our own day-to-day lives. *The Hours* is rich, varied, and honest reading that taps into our core spiritual impulse "to be dwarfed and expanded / all at once"—embracing us when we are left in longing and even in those rare, glimmering moments where the Divine does seem to break through our mundanity and toil. I loved it!
—**MEGAN MCDERMOTT,** author of *Jesus Merch: A Catalog in Poems* (Fernwood Press) and *Woman as Communion* (Game Over Books)

Matthew J. Andrews' *The Hours* is a collection elucidating our attempts to hear a still, small voice in birdsong and thunder, to seek what can be found in ecstasy and the quotidian, to grasp the hem of a garment we know is just within reach. Andrews' images are incarnated—words becoming the flesh and blood we recognize as our own—teaching us "some things stick / around. Some things don't wash so easy." These poems call us to see and be seen as we truly are, call us to examine the lies we tell ourselves about the truths we know in our hearts, call us to consider all that could be, that is "*holy, holy, holy.*"
—**MATTHEW E. HENRY,** author of *The Third Renunciation*

Matthew J. Andrews reminds me that poetry is the language of mystery, at once able and unable to grasp more than we can imagine. In these poems, Andrews faces God and creation from all angles—praise, rage, awe, grief. *The Hours* holds faith and questions loosely and beautifully, allowing new revelations with each reading. And trust me, you'll want to reread these poems.
—**WHITNEY RIO-ROSS,** author of *Birthmarks* and poetry editor of *Fare Forward*

Poetry is always worship. What makes Andrews unusual in our generation is his setting aside of idols and reaching out for God directly. And the great surprise is that He is right there. He is right there. And that is what this collection offers.

—**THERIC JEPSON,** editor of *Quatrain.Fish* and *Irreantum*

THE HOURS

Poems

Matthew J. Andrews

THE HOURS

Matthew J. Andrews

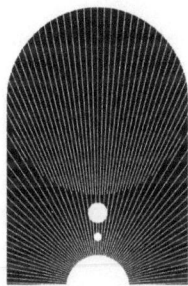

SOLUM
LITERARY PRESS

Anaheim, CA • solumpress.com

©Matthew J. Andrews, 2025

Solum Literary Press
2205 W Broadway Ave A-119
Anaheim, CA 92804

solumpress.com

PAPERBACK ISBN 978-1-965169-04-9
EBOOK ISBN 978-1-965169-05-6

Cover art and design by Sarah Christolini.
Interior design by Riley Bounds.
Author photo by Giana Silva. Used with permission.

LIBRARY OF CONGRESS CATALOGUING-IN-PUBLICATION DATA
Name: Andrews, Matthew J, author.
Title: The hours / matthew j andrews.
Description: Anaheim, CA: Solum Literary Press, 2025.
Identifiers: LCCN 2024942693
ISBN: 978-1-965169-04-9 (print)
ISBN 978-1-965169-05-6 (Kindle)
Subjects: BISAC: POETRY / American - General / Subjects & Themes - Motivational & Inspirational / Subjects & Themes - Religious
LC record available at https://lccn.loc.gov/2024942693

As for me, I call to God,
and the LORD saves me.
Evening, morning and noon
I cry out in distress,
and he hears my voice.
—Psalm 55:16–17

Each day is a little life, and our whole life is but a day repeated.
—Joseph Hall

CONTENTS

SEXT

VESPERS

THE HOURS

The Hours

The monk overcome with lusts—crumbled stone,
lingering sun, flesh bursting into flames.
And yet: there he is, body bent at each clanging bell.
It's true the slow drip that nourishes the root
also rattles the mind, that in silence the devil
too can be heard most clearly. And yet: knees
ground to powder, sweat dripping like blood.
The body a cage, the abbey a prison, the frantic soul
pacing grooves in the dirt floor. And yet:
clenched eyelids. And yet: labored breaths. And yet:

VIGILS

Are your wonders known in the place of darkness,
or your righteous deeds in the land of oblivion?
—Psalm 88:12

There Is No Such Thing as Moonlight

It's just the sun's dim residue, what's left
over after it's been choked by horizon.

But we love a good duality:
supreme light to govern the day,

lesser one for the night.
We gain power over what we name,

make it a reflection—
that slithering sound in our ears

the hiss of our own tongue.
I don't think I have it in me

to kill a man, but maybe I could
if I called him something else.

Bedtime

I rock with the boat as we read together,
waters darkened by the spilling of ink,
skies covered in clouds of scraped charcoal,

yet the faster I turn the pages, the more it animates
the waves. I tread carefully, pronouncing
each word to conceal its depth, dancing like rain

on the frothing ocean, drowning the voices
of millions of unseen faces. My daughter
spots the dove—whitewashed feathers, peace

carted in its mouth—and says *what a beautiful
bird*. I close my eyes, kiss her head, hold her
close: *yes, my love, it's a very beautiful bird.*

Strangers

Where I come from, every window
was a mirror, all the lights smothered
under layers of clouds. I long to know
where you're from. We light a candle
and watch the shadows rorschach
across the walls. I take off my shirt
and it's a briar patch. Under your robe
is another robe. Our faces: blanketed
by the darkness of the other's. Did your house
have termites, the buzzing of their jaws
audible only in the quietest moments?
We fuck like animals: with teeth exposed
and hairs raised at attention. We blow
out the candle, let the smoke hover
like a fog, wrap ourselves in it. Do you
also see your face in the clarity of night?
Do you too hear gnawing in your chest?

Hermeneutical Spiral

He draws a tunnel of constricting coils,
at the center writes: *truth*.
I turn my worn Bible upside down

in the bathtub, let it fill with ink,
watch letters swirl in a tightening pillar—
their bleeding, dark; the drain, darker still.

Gilroy

You can smell it on the city's breath
a long way off. It hits you
the moment you drop into the valley
though miles of hushed farmland

separate you from the nondescript
factories where garlic cloves are crushed,
chopped, mashed, or otherwise mutilated
in some fashion. My father,

lifetimes ago, emerged from buildings
like these, buried under a black sky,
the smell clinging to his shirt fibers
and cloth car seats, the lining

of rubber boots, a pungent curse
that followed him home and lingered
despite steamy water aimed to cleanse.
I can smell it still, in the mouth

of a stranger, in the night
air of the countryside, sometimes
on my own skin. Some things stick
around. Some things don't wash so easy.

Sundays

In the morning,
I sat and stared
at the messiah,
and her fingers snapped
if I looked away.

Under midday sun,
a sermon: her
right hand holding a chisel,
her left fingers vise-
gripping my hair.

All afternoon, she
cried as the house swamped,
and I pumped cloudy
water in the gutter
as the sun drowned.

At night, she
prowled while I, wide-
eyed in bed, wondered
if I wanted to go
to heaven after all.

Isaac at Twilight

Living in inherited land,
the setting sun

made mountains appear
to him as daggers,

and in the growing darkness,
the begetting pain of memory,

he imagined the cold
clench of steel

in his own fingers,
hovering over the pounding

heartbeat breaths
of his child.

Holy Ground

With every hellscape of wildfire,
        before flames consume

cities and return them to dust,
        before empires of green

turn to charcoal in the blaze,
        before the mouths of the living

choke on the ashes of the dead,
        there is always one wayward man,

barefoot, who waltzes
        into the newborn inferno,

burning on yet a single bush,
        and demands to hear God's voice.

Another Failed Prophecy

. . . a pyrocumulonimbus from the Loyalton wildfire is capable of pro-
ducing a fire induced tornado.—National Weather Service bulletin,
August 15, 2020

It's almost too much to believe:
that the sky—that black-mass congregation
of clouds, crackling communion
of vapor and light; that thunderclap
ejector of the uncontainable, the yearning
rebellion that drops in forked tongues,
its path illuminated like a falling star's,
its collision birthing spark and flame;
that dark courtyard pulsating with fire
and judgment—would reach back down
and summon its outcast again, its wind fingers
plucking and lifting the exiled inferno
into the air, drawing it up in swirling dance.
But when the morning comes, it's the same
as it ever was: molten sun hiding
behind smoky skies, ash falling like manna.

On the Bosphorus

I am nowhere   but I am here,

on this vessel   of tired pilgrims,

our feet unsteady   from the rocking

of this demarcation,   coffee cups sloshing

as an echo, gray   sky denying us guidance

of the sun. All   is unmoored, yet we

are bodies anchored   in stillness, breaths

of air gripped   tightly in the chest.

Minarets like ramparts   on each shoreline

call to prayer,   their music hovering

over the waters   like a mist,

but each open eye   in our weary heads

is a compass   spinning in circles.

We no longer   know which way

we are supposed   to be praying.

Submerged

Like a tadpole,
you make a home
in this fiefdom
of murky water,
this swaddling current,
vision so clouded
that tugging fingers
wrapped up in your hair
seem like leeches
sucking at the scalp.

Unfinished Psalms From the Private Notebook of King David

I praise you in psalms,
in words I shape from dust,
in songs I form from air.

How much longer until
this praise becomes worship?

When will they bloom
like flowers in your light?

*

I hear her singing,
her flesh calling to me,
a lone voice at night:
a howling wolf,
a talking fire.

Her skin like olive oil,
her breasts like pomegranates,
her body a ripe fruit
sagging on the branches,
drawing close to my lips.

*

A drunk man collapses on the street—
face dirty, robe torn,

the crowd shamed at his disgrace—
and awakens to gold coins laid out for him.

Such is this crown you have bestowed.

*

 take my baths on the roof,
washing myself in the blood.

I feel her eyes watching,
seeing my nakedness.

Vulture-priests circle
over heavy altar.

I will accept no offering
that costs her nothing.

*

Speak to me, please,
in a tone that is not thunder,
in a voice that is not rain.

*

The comfort of wine on the lips,
the warmth of her breast in my mouth;

both liven the blood like fire
but leave ash on the tongue.

*

The swords of my enemies—
Saul, my lord! Absalom, my son!—
plunge into the flesh,
my blood falling like tears.

I am losing perspective,
my nightmares and lusts
forged into a golden calf.

*

This thorn in my side—
is this your weapon?

This woman in my eye—
is this your accuser?

*

I feel you closest to me
when I am alone in the fields,

in the rolling hills flush with green,
in the grasslands spotted with sheep,

their masses bleating exaltations,
your sky accepting them with joy.

*

Sheol, this graveyard woman,
dances in my court.

Her body like sunset,
her hips rise like stars
guiding me to my bed.
I am drunk with her lips,

with the condensation of her psalms,
and I follow her into darkness.

Apollyon

Each morsel of sweetness—
pinprick on the tongue.
They came in a swarm, a cloud
pillaring down the chimney,
coating the walls, my skin,
buzzing like a dentist's hands.
Nothing's ever felt as heavenly

as stingers thrust into the flesh,
as amber sap dripping to the floor.
In my ear, they whisper: *eat.*
My lips part and in they spill,
to drill holes in my stomach,
my throat, my tongue—blood thick
in my mouth but it tastes just like honey.

Wormwood

Then it's meant to be a punishment:
this brief separation of the soul
and the throbbing weight of its return.

Fire on the tongue for the burning
in my stomach. Each night it rains,
but still more stars than I can count.

And, oh, those wonders of heaven: trumpet
blasts, piss in the river, broken bottles
pressed against my outstretched neck.

Psalm

Lord, rescue me from the jackals
encircling my house, but please, let me
keep the bones lodged in my teeth.
Am I doing this right? Does the stench
of my breath rise any higher
than my nose? This is a town
where we dump bodies in the well
and drink blood from our taps,
where our flags name no country
because they're always half-mast,
where the earth itself groans
like the want of our stomachs.
We don't deserve to be saved.
Let the jackals brandish their teeth.

Desolation Wilderness

In my dream I'm another man:
light wave curved over the earth,
shadow-self cast long by the sun.
When I step out of the tent,

into the deceiving chill of October,
there are stars speckled like glitter,
little cracks on the porous edge of darkness
where the light of another world
seeps through like a finger outstretched.

LAUDS

Satisfy us in the morning with your unfailing love,
that we may sing for joy and be glad all our days.
—Psalm 90:14

Stumbling Upon Akeldama in Winter

Empty lot: cursed
soil burned black
by raging fires
of summer sun, parched
as a dead man's lips. Yet

winter rains bring thick
skin of green, moist
breath of grasses, fluttering
heartbeat of insect wings,
and their echoing hymn:

Nothing dead must
stay that way.
Morning light brings
night's decay.

The Morning I Lived

My fingers interlocked with yours / gravity-drawn to my neck / *slow descent of your head to me* / *honeycomb sticky on your lips* / compression, suffocation / nails digging deep into my own skin / *song lowered softly to my ear* / *scent of ripened fruit on your breath* / you trapped under my crushing weight / *the way your hands opened like blossoms*

Sinner

Forgive me, Father, for I have spent hours
sitting beside an alpine lake,
staring at reflections
of mountaintops. I have retreated
to the company of ancient trees
only to lose myself tracing the ivory frame
of a deer in the dirt with my fingers.

I have held trails accountable
for their maps, tides for their charts.
I have photographed vistas but not sketched them.
I have walked blindly
past endless fields of wildflowers.
I have wasted time following the sinking sun,
counting down every hour until darkness.

Standiford Park

The men, nowhere to go, set up tents
at the fence line, under the shade of oak
trees and the Orthodox church standing

on the other side of the ivy-covered barrier.
They pass cigarettes, jostle for space,
talk loudly like old friends,

but they are quiet when the chanting
begins, and even though none speak Greek,
they feel the words of the incantation

move like brushfire in their bones
and watch them dance in swirling currents
as they rise into the sky like smoke.

I'm Not Sure I Have Ever Prayed

but I have spent hours of every day
meditating in the shadow of prayers unsaid,
in the petitions and praises that hover untethered
in my mind like leaves in the wind.
I have felt their ghosts breathing on my neck,
their whispers sending shivers down the arm.
I have seen their pale skin discarded in coils
on the floor, the body slithered away.
I have seen them melt into puddles in the heat
of darkness and lapped at them with my tongue,
like a dog, desperate for thirst.

Maundy

Miles of dirt cling
to my legs, to my feet,
as I arrive at the pool,
the natural void
filled in by the river
as it meanders down
the mountain. The water meditates
in stillness. The sky is a deep
cerulean, bannered by white
strips of clouds. I remove
my shoes and place my feet
in the water, and the alpine
chill pierces the skin
as it cleanses. I sit
for a long time, swishing
my feet in circles, before I
notice the thistle whiplashes
on the arm, the salt collection
scattered on the forehead,
the dull ache echoing
under the skin. I remove
the rest of my clothes, stand
naked under the warm sun
of summer, look down
into the bottomless basin,
and close my eyes as I jump,
the fall like an eternity.

Annunciation

A swooping hawk, Gabriel descends
to a barren, unexpectant earth,
his feathers a train of candles
settled in a prolonged burn.
Mary receives him, a haloed
icon, the patron saint of contradiction:
the body recoils, the womb drawn
to the comfort of the dirt,
yet her hands cradle the child,
that fire burning at her breast.
Her eyes meet the angel's,
the duality of their gaze locked
like the door just moments ago.

more

each year, i want
more of it

bigger canvasses
in one shade of blue

infinity symbols
in larger font

acres of white space
across the page

a sky
so vast and cloudless

i am dispersed
under its crushing weight

to be dwarfed and expanded
all at once

so much breath
in my lungs

that i am
breathless

Embryo

I tap an egg three times
on the counter before I crack
it open. Not sure why.

It's not some subtle
reminder of the loved ones
I encase in my shell,

not some Trinitarian tribute
to a body broken for me.
It's just something I do

because I did it before,
perhaps years ago,
and found a clean break,

graceful sliding of yolk.
Science will tell us
this is nonsense,

a malfunction in the brain
raising a picture to the eye
when there are only scattered points,

but maybe there's some magic in us,
the way we stack three stones
and call them a temple,

the way we knock three times
on every wall
and call it a door.

Guardian Angel

Mine is a manna-spirit, a holy being
with an apron tied around its waist,
who finds me when I am aimless
and gently places my hands in the muck,

forcing me to work with my fingers
until I have something resembling solidity,
a tacky ball of clay, and then to knead,
to pound and pull it into a resilient

mass that clings to its shape. The angel
then sits me down, teaches me to breathe
in slow rhythms like lapping ocean waves
as we wait. All day long it's rest

and work, cyclical patterns of reflection
and activity, a death preceding a birth.
Finally, there is the purification of fire.
At the end, the angel shows me

the hardened shell, and buried under,
a holy meal, airy and soft, with spirit-
swelled pockets of smoke and breath:
a Sabbath gift, a harvest for my toil.

Endless

1.

Crack the earth open like an egg
and watch magma spill out as yolk.

Rip a lamb apart like a loaf of bread
and watch the innards tumble as seeds.

To seek is nothing more than to lust
for dissection, the opening of flesh like a door,

and to mourn when it is yet another hallway,
another stack of boulders awaiting dynamite.

Cut the straps that hold your body together
and watch another you emerge from the rubble,

and from him, another, each
a little less runny, each a little more clear.

2.

Pilgrim breath
kneels, bows, settles
into a rhythm of prayer,
of repetitive incantation—
fill me,
be filled by me.

The temple lungs swell
and retract with the words,
echoing them back,
emitting them through open windows
like smoke from a candle.

The wine ripples
when the heart pitches
like a tuning fork.

Each half of lamb
bleats back at the other.

3.

As we are commissioned,
we bury both parts of the lamb
in the dirt, put our lips
against the soil, and pray
as the corpse nourishes.

As we are commanded,
we splinter the staff over our knees,
sprinkle shards on the soil,
and watch as a tree emerges,
branches sagging with fruit, golden
like a king's crown,
and then we take and we eat.

Wonderful Counselor

Each session is the same:
the cushion buckles under my weight,
bricks crumble out of my mouth,
the room clouds with dust.

You sit and listen,
nodding like a bird, lips
pursed in silent song, soft
cursive soaring across a page.

When I am done, you lean in close,
the wind of your breath in my hair,
and ask me once again: *have you
thought any more about flying?*

Mt. Jurupa

Near the summit, above the smog
this mountain wears like a sash,
a technicolor Jesus is painted
on a granite canvass, arms expanded
in welcome to weary pilgrims,
in presentation of the land below:
vast spread of concrete scars,
hazy square plots, tiny men
grained like sand—His kingdom,
His children, His sermon crying out
from the stones, perforating my silence.

Birdsongs

1.

I came back to the place,
found only a flock of doves

pecking at scraps in the street,
cooing in communion.

Was that you speaking?

2.

I have read that bird colonies
can be millions strong, a mass
of squawking everlasting.

Yet amidst the cacophony, a child
always knows the mother's call,
can always pick it out,

can always be fed.

3.

I'm trying to write a gospel
of bird noises, but I'll be damned
to make any sense of them.

The sounds are simple,
but the tones shift,
the pitches undulate.

It's impossible to know whether each trill
is admonishment or admiration,
whether the barely whispered *cooooo*
is the tenderness of a lover's kiss
or the quiet mourning of a broken heart.

4.

The voice erupts, an atom
bomb in the sky, whipping

clothes in its wind, drawing blood
from ruptured eardrums.

There is nothing like it. The closest
you can get on your own

is to jam quill pens
in the ears:

flagellation of words,
auditory stigmata,

imitation of birdsong.

Sutter Buttes

Craggy ramparts conceal a grander truth:
all things end where they begin. Every line
curves back on itself and encircles
a center, soft and peaceful.
Ask the vulture for its eyes
and you will see it.

Supernova

It will be eight minutes
before we know of it.

We'll be out in the wilderness
on a spring afternoon,

watching the flowers open
themselves as wide as possible

while the frenzied cloud of bees
reaps this new harvest.

Eight minutes of rising heat.
We'll feel it spread on our skin

and welcome its stroke.
The clothes will vanish

like the last of night's dew,
and we'll lie down together

on a verdant bed of living
things, sweat moistening

the places where we touch,
steam escaping our open mouths.

It will end as it all began:
two lovers uniting in flesh,

eyes closed to the radiance
burning at the garden's edge.

SEXT

For day and night
your hand was heavy on me;
my strength was sapped
as in the heat of summer.
—Psalm 32:4

Imagine Jesus Lives a Long Life

He keeps his feet on the ground
and his eyes out of the sky so he can see
clearly the details of his work: the nails
held lightly in the fingers as the hammer falls.

He avoids crowds, spending much of his time
alone in his shop, sanding and carving. *God
is not the clouds*, he tells the men
who seek him out. *He is*

*in every swirling grain of cedar, every speck
of sawdust, every splinter under the skin.
Every hand's a priest, each work an offering.*
The devil visits often as the years amass,

watching with pity as his eyesight fades,
as his fingers wilt and curl inwards,
as death spreads slowly through his veins.
I can heal you, the devil says, hand extended,

face flushed of malice, *I can make you young.*
But Jesus only smiles and shakes his head:
*Give a man enough time, old friend,
and he can learn to endure almost anything.*

Pebbles in the Spillway

My grandfather's house: a menagerie
of working-class wonder, an Eden
crafted of spare parts, the smell
of grease and sawdust hovering.

Scrap metal reborn as scales, abaci,
Morse code transmitters. Wine
from neglected fruits: bananas, plums, cherries.
Shiny bowls of harvested abalone.

Hanging from the ceiling were mobiles,
puppet-string planets twirling in orbit,
each body a pebble so perfectly round
it would make a mathematician weep.

He taught us that rocks get caught in spillways
of dams and pummeled by merciless waters
until softened and smoothed into circles:
a rough refinement on that narrow path.

Father's Day

I shave my face
with Abraham's knife,

just the way he taught me,
scraping the soft skin

with the edge of the blade.
Each year I am better

at not cutting myself,
but I am far from perfect,

the instrument much too sharp,
the flesh so swollen with blood.

Upon Seeing a Pomegranate Orchard

I can't help but think of our ancient parents
contending with their garden, their hands
scarred and calloused from work, their brows

slick with perspiration, every speck of skin
hardened with grime from hundreds of years
of toiling, watching, waiting, all to find

barren branches sagging only with failure,
year after year, no holy water to moisten
their roots, until finally ruby fruits appeared

like gems on their limbs, and upon plucking
one and ripping it apart with weathered hands,
there were seeds more numerous than stars

spilling outwards, oozing red like shed blood,
and the pleasing thought: *I made this myself.*

Hunger

If we are a little lower than angels,
we are not much higher than beasts,

simple creatures who worship our hungers,
flesh that lusts for things to be consumed.

I sometimes imagine Jesus in the wilderness,
frail as any man: withering slowly to dust,

stomach collapsing in ruins, aromas
of temptation wafting in the lonely desert sky.

How much harder those lingering days
must have been than his climactic one,

when the pain, so acute and overwhelming,
was only temporary, one last obstacle

between the primitive suffering of incarnation
and the waiting arms of glory.

Out there in the empty land, the cross
a lifetime away, subject to the animal

instincts of his creation, the temporal
desires of a human body, a small concession

in exchange for the soft relief of bread
must have sounded like a hell of a deal.

Orchard

Homogeny's an insatiable god.
Trees line up like bar codes.

We cut the throats of our children,
turn their necks into canals.

A teardrop splatters the roots.
The tree quivers. We open our mouths.

Hermitage

I wash dishes: one
plate, one fork, one cup.

Burnt orange sunrise
tangles in tree limbs.

On the wall: Christ,
inanimate; a cardinal, still.

The trees lean together,
bowing to the east.

I take a walk, to vanish,
but I'm still right here.

Am I My Brother's Keeper?

The question spills out
the fracture of my mouth
like juice from the cracked flesh
of a pomegranate,
running down the trunk
of my body, dampening dirt
like morning dew.

How loud does blood speak?
How well does its voice carry?
If it cries from soil, amplified
by the wind, can its plea
be heard through hospital doors,
through the thick walls of trucks
cooled to hold corpses?

A rock in the hand is a prism,
a coagulation of dust, a dense
ball of matter waiting to explode
into a universe of our choosing,
awaiting only a word
to come dripping from our lips.

Reaping & Sowing in a Minefield

The field, still and breathless,
colored in thirsty hues of yellow,
sits beneath hills just as bleak,
the whole land scoured in disinfectant

and scrubbed clean of stains,
a Lady Macbeth at her basin.
Yet nothing buried stays dormant:
the seeds germinate and expand,

the tendrils pulled up towards sunlight,
until the bursting of ripe fruit
cracks like a distant gunshot,
like blood crying out from the dirt.

Sentence

Take the words of the Lord, the statutes and commandments He dropped to earth like an anchor, and write them on the walls, one verse at a time, until your house is a confession. Etch them onto your skin, in a helix over hands and arms, until scarring elevates each word. Paint them on the inside of your eyelids, bright enough so they illuminate as lightning when you blink. Write them outside: with dead leaves on the lawn, hot urine in the snow, crab shells on the shore. Arrange the clouds as a testimony, drops of rain as a witness. Teach psalms to the birds so it's a constant choir as you walk. Form them in the stars, read until you fall asleep, and flood your dreams with incantation, an endless rehearsal for the day when you will be swept up into the text, one black dot in letters spilled across a sentence.

Jonah and the King

Of course I doubted him: crazed man
of dust blown in by wind, waterlogged
eyes, salt baked onto his skin, demanding

penance in the name of a god foreign
to my ears, telling stories dripping wet
with madness. But he took my hand

with surprising strength and guided
my fingers down the length of his arm,
to the wounds riddling him like pockmarks,

those places where the grave's teeth tore
into the skin, and to the patches burned
with the corrosive splash of Sheol's stomach,

and as I imagined the pain his god
had made him endure, he drew my eyes
up to his and asked me: *do you now believe?*

Table Rock

I see the exposed face of granite,
flat as a dead man's heart,
rise up as an altar
and imagine climbing, hands
grasping towards the heavens
with sharpened stone shards
to make offerings
of unblemished clouds.

The wind whispers:
do you do well
to be angry?

An Activist's Diary

October 8th

Approaching on angel's wings,
I see the sky seem to stretch forever,
pillowy clouds, the sun as close
as a lemon at arm's reach.

When we descend, the heavens collapse
into land where the color
has been drained
like fruit shriveled
in the heat.

*

October 9th

In the city's lone church,
only a few congregate
behind sturdy brick walls,
the sisters reciting prayers
in the same language Jesus used
when he said:

Thy kingdom come

It is finished

*The axe is already
at the root of the tree*

*

October 10th

The walls of the memorial
are glass, smashed and fractured,
each shard a dead soul,
each of us a thousand shards,
the sharp edges traced
with our splintered fingers.

*

October 11th

Why can't you stop killing each other?
I ask everyone I meet,

but their faces are blank,
each mouth a cavern,
every response an echo.

*

October 12th

The old-timers
teach us the golden rule:
Whoever is not against us is for us.

But the cracks in the earth
add their wisdom:
Every handshake is with the devil
if you hold tight enough.

*

October 13th

The lake nestled in the desert
mountains is a bed of crystal,
an arctic blue that shows each rock
its true face, every cloud its soul.

I look into it and see nothing.

*

October 14th

Nothing disappoints
like mixing your tears
with sand to make clay,
then forming it
into a thing you can worship,
which always resembles
something out of reach:
lion, stork,
father, son,
demon, angel.

*

October 15th

Somewhere in the bleached hills
that form the hazy border between states,
amidst rocks littered on treeless slopes,
lies what's left of my corpse,
sunken flesh gouging my face,
heart already plucked by vultures.

*

October 16th

Long ride to the airport
and I'm thinking about the fig
I had that morning, plucked
from the tree in the courtyard,
the diamond-dusted sweetness
dancing on my tongue, praying:
Let not every tree wither under your breath.

No Snakes in Ireland

St. Patrick stands at the shore:
slithered impressions in the sea,
smile smeared on his lips,
staff slurred into a half circle.

Angels soaring in the Irish sky
listen to the hiss of ocean
waves, trace with their fingers
the serpentine shape of coastline.

Autobiography of a Private Investigator

I

More than the illicit activities I'm hired to observe, it's the little things that stick with me about people who don't know they're being watched: the unsucked guts, the saggy breasts, the disheveled faces, the limp way their limbs move about, the itching, the fidgeting, the lips moving in silent rehearsals, the way they stare blankly into the distance as they nurse a cigarette. I find myself wondering: is God this bored and this titillated all at the same time?

II

The science is bullshit. Lying eyes don't look up and to the left. Tremoring fingers are indicative of nothing. Everyone lies all the time, every breath inhaling truth and exhaling perversion. Shine a light into their disco-ball mouths and watch them shade reality into sparkling hues, spraying it all over the walls as they dance to the rhythm of their own falsehood, lost in the beat. No wonder Pilate washed his hands—you don't get answers without breaking some legs.

III

I once spent hours on TikTok downloading videos of a man claiming be injured, gyrating his girth to music, slamming his body against the wall, putting knife blades between his fingers, all the while begging, *I will eat shit, I will jump off this roof, I will crash my car, just like me, just follow me.* People are not watches buried in the sand. They are not pearls trapped in clamshells. They are open wounds, pussy and festering, giving you a good look at their inner workings. They have machinery that hums too loud. They couldn't hide if they wanted to.

IV

I once met the devil in an airport bar, and we spent hours talking down whiskey glasses in that modern purgatory. He asked me if I liked what I did, and after thinking about it, I told him it had its moments of fun, but that there were also days that drained the soul of everything it had, that ultimately it didn't matter whether I liked it or not because it was a job like any other, and if someone has to do it, it may as well be me. The devil chuckled and raised his glass to me: *Amen, brother. Amen.*

A New Parable

It's a heavy burden, to decide
how much meaning to give a day,
to discern whether time is sand
slipping through fingers
or glass shredding skin.
Yes, I've heard the stories—
virgins with no oil,
servant with booze on his breath
and blood on his knuckles—
but have you heard the one where bombs
rain like sulfur from the sky,
where the earth parches and shrivels,
where we turn ourselves inside out
and turn each other into mirrors,
and all the while a man walks quietly
and watches a bird flitter between branches
as dusk begins its steady march,
wondering if anyone is coming to take
our bleeding hands, or if it's just us,
these birds, this fire, that swelling darkness?

Work Song

City birds seldom call out in song.
They speak in utilitarian chirps,
a squawking vernacular to guide
them on their morning commutes—
wire to branch, branch to dirt,
dirt to highway of cloudy skies—
the way we mumble to each other
about open seats on the bus,
our heads bobbing with the staccato
rhythm of halt and motion, mouths hungry
for crumbs scattered on the street.
Yet even then there are moments,
small moments late in the day
when the drumbeat of sledge
on steel brings to the lips a tune
our mothers used to whistle
in the kitchen as they worked,
their knuckles kneaded and buckled
but their mouths high in the clouds,
soaring on wingspreads of air,
and we softly sing their memories
to the waving branches of the trees
and listen as the birds sing back.

VESPERS

My days are like the evening shadow;
I wither away like grass.
—Psalm 102:11

Introduction to Astrology

It's because of the planets and stars,
she explains, their arrangement
in the sky at the exact moment of my birth,
that I am me, their unique swirl of gravities

responsible for the shape of my longings.
Pagan nonsense, my father would say,
as would the long line of fathers before him,
each now dissolved to the dust at our feet.

Our God created the heavens, endless spread
of suns reaching across an infinite horizon,
to display like cosmic artwork
high above the grasp of dirty fingers.

But why should such glory be wasted?
Why shouldn't the stars pull at our bodies,
tugging our atoms apart ever so slightly
until we're constellations on this earth?

And why shouldn't they reclaim us at death,
drawing the wisdom of our stardust
into themselves so they can burn ever
stronger for the children who come next?

Patmos

It is here, under the heavy blanket of silence
that accompanies exile, the body cut

into patterns by the skin wrinkled with age,
that he finally understands how one can be

surrounded by life, in a garden of ancient trees swaying
in the wind and flowers opening themselves

to the beckoning of sun, and be so empty.
How one can look up at the star-speckled

heavens and see the shapes of prowling beasts,
floodlit by the fire on the horizon.

How one can stack stones into temples,
blood on the brow, eyes red with grief,

and imagine what it is to be reborn
to give birth to something new.

First Night in Iowa

Cicadas blared like sirens,
in the trees shouting *theft*.

On Nebraskan plains,
on the slopes of the Rockies,

people opened their doors,
gawked eastward to find

branches trembling
like shattered glass.

We stepped out, saw
only sound rattling leaves

against the night sky,
felt the noise sharp

in the bowls of our ears.
We stood there for hours,

eyes straining in the dark.
Alarms never tell you

what's missing. They only
announce that it's gone.

Nod

I've walked a long way east
and now the trees are all on fire,

tremoring flames in the wind.
Autumn chill in the air,

and true to its name, the locust
drops all its leaves at once,

each a flickering candlewick.
It's beautiful, but so are most curses.

I hear them crunch under my feet
but can't feel them through the blisters.

I try to pray, but
my mouth is packed with dirt.

In a moment, every branch is barren,
pointing fingers in the fading light.

All Fallen Leaves Must Curse Their Branches

But it's in their nature to fall,
the leaves and the men watching,

to drink in deep and rust,
to unclasp and decompose.

This is not profound, yet my father
sews his eyes shut in autumn,

strips naked and flitters
beneath a vanishing sun, resentment

he refuses to name pumping
through his ever-reddening heart.

Curse the branches? I've lost count
of the things that have dropped me,

thickened my stomach to brace against
the disorientation of gravity.

To curse them is to choke
on feathers, to asphyxiate

while stray ones waft in the breeze
and drop slowly to the dirt.

There is no saving them, no saving yourself.
Look up and watch the rustling inferno,

let each little flame land on your palm,
and let it be extinguished.

Coram Deo

I catalogue my heresies on the bar,
lay them out like empty glasses. *This is holy,*
you tell me, and I laugh because it feels
like a swollen leech calling itself medicine.
I'm tired of defining myself by what is lost.
You buy me another beer and say *God*
is all around, even here, between us like a mist,
and I laugh because on the horizon flames
exhale their toxic cloud of ash and smoke.
I'm tired of every breath shredding the walls
of my lungs. You tell me *everyone feels lost.*
I don't laugh because for once I don't doubt,
and we take slow sips of the following pause.
I close my eyes, let myself bathe in sound:
drinks clinking as rosary beads, words folded
together in a murmur of prayer, and loudest
of all, laughter, cutting sharp like shattered glass.

Whole and Entire

Instead of consolidated on heaven's throne,
the multiplicitous body of Christ
fractures: the dour one with closed

eyes, displayed on church walls—
bloodied, slumped, wordless; the one
chopped like onions and presented

by a priest, who places the dissolvent
flesh on the tongue; the discorporate
one lining pews and aisles, feet

shuffling, hands folded, mouths agape—
pilgrim parts longing for a form to embody,
for a skin to wear draped like a robe.

The God of Broken Things

In the beginning, there was garbage:
planks of wood from rotten bedframes,
frayed wires, scraps of paper.

The firstborn creation: a splinter
lodged into my hand, tears of blood
dripping from the pulsing wound.

Priests with torn clothing and matted hair
tend to the altar, bring their gifts
of food wrappers and shattered glass.

Each night we light it on fire
and bring our heads to the ground
as the voice declares: *holy, holy, holy.*

Confession

The angel who talked with me had a measuring rod of gold to measure the city, its gates and its walls. —Revelation 21:15

When it's all over, when what's left
of the world sizzles with flame
and the line to hell snakes for miles
like the opening of a roller coaster,
the holy men will be on hands and knees,
holding rulers against jasper walls.

Fellow pilgrim, will you hear my confession?
I no longer measure once, twice,
a thousand times in hopes the blade
will miss my flesh when it slices.
I throw garlic in the pan with abandon.
I let the watch die on the grave of my wrist
and fall asleep when my body tells me to.
I cover my speedometer with duct tape
and drive for hours with the windows down.

Dear pilgrim, if one day you find me
shuffling along with those who've fallen short,
can you take your ruler and calculate
the distance between us? Can you tell it
to God himself and then measure his arms?

Peter Goes Fishing on the Sea of Tiberias

The fishing is hard with the constant
lapping of rooster crows at the boat,
the trawler weighted with dredged feathers.

Peter watches the shoreline, thinks about how
rocks are just sand not yet subjected
to the eroding forces of wind,

how the land is just a vacuum
not yet filled by water. On the beach,
there is a fire burning with smoke

signals rising in pillars, a man
crouched beside it, morning sun
reflecting off the sword at his side.

Peter knows the man, has always
known the man, as if the moth
could ever forget the call of the flame.

He steps over the side, places his foot
on the water, and walks to shore,
buoyant, weightless. The sword unsheathes

and summons by name. He closes his eyes,
feels the steel at his neck, determined,
for once, to be faithful to something.

Cathedrals

We are sober tonight, and our love is gentle, unhurried, each motion deliberate and euphoric, as if we're wandering for the first time into a temple where everything's coated in gold. I've been thinking lately about vacations we'll never take: sunsets in Patagonia, frolics in wine country, long hikes between distilleries in the Highlands. Each a drop seeping through the cracks, landing at the bottom of a glass. I'm drowning in sensation: the dampness of your breath, your sweat slick against mine, the bouquet of flavors on my tongue. We hold each other like we never want to let go, dreading the moment the sun will rise and life will pry away our fingers. There are churches in Ethiopia we will never see that are dug into the ground, holy places of stone that dare to stand in defiance of death. Maybe there are cathedrals below us waiting to be uncovered. The dirt is dry, my love. We can dig.

Capela dos Ossos

The risen Christ stands magnetic
at the chapel's center,
preaching to an audience of bleached bones,

words reverberating off solemn ivory
walls and the cavities within them,
former housings for eyes, for ears.

Grooved pieces of macabre masonry
present history in stratal columns,
fate in arches layered like tree rings:

you are, and then you are not,
the flesh evaporated like vapor,
the remaining dust petrified to wisdom

and stacked high into an altar,
a beacon for skin and bone.

New Years

In that peculiar way
a stranger
becomes a lover
in the fog
of a dream,
this road escapes
the low cloud
and finds morning
kiss of sun,
spread of blue sky.
You know this can't last,
that the road
rises and drops
like tired bodies
in church pews,
but for this moment,
this sliver of clarity,
it can be enough
to drive
just a little further.

Fall Storm

Every year, more ash
accumulates in my hair,

the way leaves gather
in corners where wind is trapped.

A tree loses its majesty
when ravaged:

bones with no flesh,
ivory shriveled and parched,

kindling for the hearth.
The flickering hounds of hell

will have their meal,
will lick the plate clean.

Come: take my hand.
Walk with me into the dark night

of heaven's shadow.
Let us drink from the vessel

while there's life left in it,
while it still spills from the sky.

Thanksgiving

It's an inherited error of perspective
that we think the bread has been changed,
transformed as some sort of magic trick,
when it is us who eventually change: mouths open
as a creaky door, inside a steady fire,
heat coaxing grain to molt and take flight.
So it is with our rituals.

Each year we form a circle, hands held
like a séance, and repeat as mantra
that we are grateful for all of it,
even the long silences spanning the gap
between two ends of a telephone,
the fence posts and roof tiles sprinkled
over the plains like salt when the winds have died,

the evening mist of tears on the pillow.
Though the words echo like knuckles
rapping against a hollow wall, we say them still,
each repetition the lacing of fingers,
the lighting of a candle, the bruising
of a knee against the floor—the longing
for incarnation to seep into our breath.

At a Photography Exhibition by Teenage Afghan Refugees

Hot coffee, Styrofoam cups,
cookies laid out in rows,
easels arranged in a circle,
as if around a campfire.

*

Image one: bright yellow
sunflowers, heads high,
lattice-shadowed by chain link.

*

One man remarks, *This is so cliché.*
The young artist does not hear him;
she is deep in conversation with a woman
fighting back tears. The man throws
his white cup away, half empty.

*

Another image: a butterfly
punches its way out
of a cocoon prison.

*

I remember no names
or titles, but I remember
the artist
alternating his weight
from one leg to another,
his right hand holding
the left in front of him,
his work standing
by his side, up to his shoulders
like a younger brother.

*

His piece: budded branches
of a tree sneak like secrets
through a slat in a wooden gate
and bloom.

*

Every artist statement: a murder.
The walk between each one: a mourning.
Their accumulation: a massacre.

*

Another: a garden with colors
from every edge of the spectrum.
Or so you imagine. The photograph
is washed of color, leaving only
light and its shadow.

*

I remember I once learned
cliché was coined
by French printmakers,
who derived it from a word
meaning "to click"
to embody the sound made

when crafted molds
were pressed down hard
into molten metal to create
a solid impression.

The critic has already left,
but he wouldn't have cared.

*

Another: a bird takes flight
next to a decrepit building. A window,
busted, shards spilled like blood,
haunts the background.

*

I lose myself imagining
my children buried under rubble
after a building has exploded
and collapsed like a dying star,
my wife dragged by her hair
from our house, bodies
piled on the street's edge like plowed snow.

*

Another: a young woman
in a hijab looks away
from the camera, facing the past, behind
her. We look with her, but we cannot
see the things she has seen,
the things she continues to see.

*

I learn the Farsi word for art: رنه.
A woman, the mother of one artist,
tells me to pronounce it by saying *honor*,
with the words coming from deep
down in my chest, near the heart.

*

Last image: the sun sets
over the valley we share, this home
of ours, the rays illuminating clear skies,
thick groves of almond trees, green
with life, a house with an open door.

Solstice

Like a carpet for the night's coronation,
fog unrolls over this city

until we are blanketed along with tree
branches and the roofs of our neighbors'

houses. Rumors of planets converging
hover in the air like mist, but even the glow

of streetlamps is swallowed. No moon
to guide us, no Christmas star

to lead the way, the children
and I move from house to house,

following the trail of twinkling lights
affixed to eaves and windowsills,

draped over lawns and fruit trees, beacons
shepherding us along each leg of the journey.

When the darkness stretches its shadow
longest, we pilgrims make our own stars.

Evening Walk in the End of Days

The highlight is the firework show of falling stars,
the way they flare up and drop in multitudes
like cosmic rain, as if darkness will never come.

When the moon rises, it's a long walk down a trail
bathed in the neon glow of a crimson halo,
the woods gently lit as if by a campfire.

Aromas of burnt wood hover, yet trees still stand in clusters,
branches stretched in scribbled shadows across the path,
psalms whispered in the rustling of leaves in the gale.

Even the bodies scattered in the dirt seem arranged
as an audience, eyes awe-opened like blooming flowers,
palms cupped as porcelain vessels, waiting in anticipation.

And why not? Isn't every evening a gift to be savored,
even the ones made darker by ash? And doesn't beauty
sparkle like starlight even when smashed into pieces?

Notes and Acknowledgments

Many thanks to the editors of the literary journals and anthologies who previously published some of these poems, sometimes in earlier versions and with different titles:

Amethyst Review, Anthology of Honest Spiritual Literature, As Surely as the Sun Literary Journal, Barren Magazine, Bez & Co., Braided Way Magazine, Collateral Journal, The Clayjar Review, Dappled Things, Deep Wild: Writing from the Backcountry, Earth & Altar, EcoTheo Review, Ekstasis, The Ethicist, Fathom Magazine, Foreshadow Magazine, Ginosko Literary Journal, Jewish Literary Journal, Kissing Dynamite, LETTERS Journal, Macrina Magazine, The Meadow, Mizmor Anthology, MockingHeart Review, Nixes Mate Review, The North American Anglican, ONE ART: a journal of poetry, Orange Blossom Review, Peatsmoke Journal, Presence: A Journal of Catholic Poetry, Reformed Journal, Rock & Sling, Rockvale Review, Rust & Moth, Saint Katherine Review, San Pedro River Review, Santa Clara Review, Second Chance Lit, Sierra Nevada Review, Sojourners, Solid Food Press Literary Journal, Solum Journal, U.S. Catholic Magazine, Vita Poetica Journal, Windhover: A Journal of Christian Literature, and *Without a Doubt: Poems Illuminating Faith.*

"Hunger," "Isaac at Twilight," "Patmos," "Peter Goes Fishing on the Sea of Tiberias," and "Unfinished Psalms From the Private Notebook of King David" were previously collected in the chapbook *I Close My Eyes and I Almost Remember.*

"Stumbling Upon Akeldama in Winter" was also collected in *An Outcast Age: An Anthology of Christian Verse.*

"At a Photography Exhibition by Teenage Afghan Refugees" was also collected in *Vultures & Doves: Social Issues of Our Time.*

The following poems were written after works in *Honest Advent* by Scott Erickson: "Annunciation" (*Annunciation*), "Endless" (*The Lamb Who Was Who Is and Who Is to Come*), and "Wonderful Counselor" (*Wonderful Counselor*).

"All Fallen Leaves Must Curse Their Branches" is after David Bazan's song of the same title.

"Jonah and the King" is after James Patrick Reid's *Jonah*.

"Whole and Entire" is after a passage in Dietrich Bonhoeffer's *The Cost of Discipleship*. ("Here he is, the same Christ whom the disciples encountered, the same Christ whole and entire.")

I am thankful for and indebted to those who provided thoughts and feedback, either on this manuscript as a whole or on some of the individual poems contained within: Riley Bounds, Joshua Andrews, Matthew E. Henry, Abbe E. Murray, and Marissa Glover.

As always, I am thankful for my family, both immediate and extended, for their love and support.

www.ingramcontent.com/pod-product-compliance
Lightning Source LLC
Chambersburg PA
CBHW030850090426
42737CB00009B/1174